The Man God Kept Surprising

Saint William of Bourges

By Susan Peek

Illustrated by Martina Parnelli

Second Edition Seven Swords Publications
ISBN: 0-9970005-5-4
ISBN-13: 978-0-9970005-5-9

Artwork © Jean Kenney

Cover Design: Theresa Linden

For ordering information, please contact:
SevenSwordsPublications@gmail.com

www.susanpeekauthor.com

For my son William, with apologies that it is years too late.
I hope you enjoy it anyhow.

And in memory of my beloved father, William Millovitsch,
whom I miss more than words can say.
I hope you're reading this over my shoulder from Heaven, Dad,
with your dear patron, Saint William, by your side.

Over eight hundred years ago, in the time of brave knights and towering castles, there lived in the country of France a boy by the name of William. His father was a nobleman and their family was very rich. Like all sons of noblemen, William learned the things he needed to know in order to be a knight someday when he grew up: how to ride a horse, how to fight a battle, how to use a sword, and lots of exciting things like that (which every boy reading this story probably wishes he could learn too!).

William also had to study normal things, like grammar and spelling and arithmetic, which aren't as exciting as riding a horse, but William didn't mind. He loved all his lessons. The subjects he loved most were the ones that taught him about God, things with big names like Theology and Sacred Scripture. He studied Latin, which is the language of the Catholic Church, and he spent many hours reading the beautiful Gospel stories and the writings of the saints.

It didn't take long for William to decide that he wanted to give his life to God and become a saint too. So that's exactly what he set out to do.

When he was old enough, he announced to his parents that he was leaving home. He was going to build for himself a little hut out in the woods, where he could live alone and pray and study as much as he wanted, without having to worry about worldly things anymore.

At first his parents were upset at this news, for they'd hoped William would become a famous knight, or a great lawyer or scholar, or choose some other job that earned a lot of money. After all, no one had ever been known to get rich by kneeling around and praying all day!

But William explained that he didn't want an important job and lots of money. He didn't care for honors and what people thought of him. All those things might make him proud. Instead, William wanted to be poor and unknown and lead a hidden life where only God would see him.

So, early one morning when the birds were chirping and the sun shining brightly, William left his father's castle and tramped off into the woods. He whistled and sang as he hiked along, his heart light and merry with a future of loving God stretching gloriously ahead of him.

When he found a suitable spot, far from the noise and bustle of the town, William got busy and built himself a hut. Now he could spend all his time alone thinking about Our Lord.

William lived in his rough little shack for several happy years, very content with the peace and quiet of the woods. He would have gladly stayed there for the rest of his life. But God had other plans for William, wonderful secret plans that William didn't know about yet . . .

One day, while William was praying, a dazzling light suddenly lit up the hut. It was so bright and beautiful that William was nearly blinded! He had to close his eyes. When he dared to open them again, he got a tremendous surprise. There, in the middle of his floor, stood Our Lord!

"My dear son William," Jesus said to him, "you have served me very well all these years here in the woods. I'm pleased by all the sacrifices and love you have given Me. But now I want you to do something different."

"Of course, Lord!" William answered eagerly. "I will do whatever Thou dost desire."

"Go then," Jesus instructed, "to the Abbey at Pontigny, and ask to become a monk there."

Pontigny was a monastery known throughout France for the holiness of its members. The monks there were called Cistercians, and they wore white habits and did lots of penance. (The most famous Cistercian of all is Saint Bernard. Maybe you have heard of him? But that is a whole separate story!)

William did as Our Lord commanded and set out at once for Pontigny. When he arrived there, the Abbot (who is the head-monk) welcomed him with joy. So William became a Cistercian and after awhile was ordained a priest.

Years went by. For the second time, William thought he would stay in this same place for the rest of his life. But God had another surprise waiting!

One day the Bishop wrote to the Abbot of Pontigny and told him to talk to William. When William came to the Abbot's door, the Abbot showed him the Bishop's letter and said, “Pack your suitcase. You're going to Fontaine.” (Fontaine was the name of another town in France.)

“Fontaine?” William asked in confusion. “Why would I want to go there?”

“Because there is another Cistercian monastery in that town,” the Abbot told him, “and their Abbot has just died. The Bishop has chosen you to be the new one.”

William was sad. The last thing in the world he wanted was to be an Abbot and be in charge of an entire monastery! He desired only to be the lowest and most forgotten monk in France.

But, in his heart, William knew that a good monk must always obey. How much God loves obedience! So he gathered his belongings (which didn't take long because Cistercians are very poor), and, putting on a brave smile, left as soon as he could for Fontaine.

William made an excellent Abbot. He was so kind and cheerful that the other monks loved him at once. He was never too busy to listen to people's problems or to offer a helping hand with the monastery chores. Being the Abbot, he didn't have to do the unpleasant jobs, like scrubbing the floors or cleaning the bathrooms. But these were the tasks which William chose to do himself, rather than make others do them. Often the Brothers would find him, his sleeves rolled up, washing the dishes or weeding the garden . . . and always with a cheerful smile on his face.

Eventually William was sent to a third monastery called Chalis, where he also served as Abbot. He thought that *surely* God would leave him here for the rest of his years. But he was wrong again. The biggest surprise of all was just around the corner.

Unknown to William, the Archbishop of a city called Bourges had recently died. The Pope needed a new Archbishop to replace him. He had heard of William's holiness and decided that this humble and cheerful Cistercian Abbot was exactly the man for the job.

A few days later, William received a message from the Pope, in which the Holy Father told him of his decision. William was to come immediately to Bourges, there to be consecrated a bishop.

Poor William shed many tears. He didn't want to become someone as important as an Archbishop! He didn't want to change his white Cistercian habit for the stark black cassock of a bishop and go back to the problems and affairs of the world. He wanted so badly to stay at his monastery with the monks he had grown to love as if they were his true brothers.

At first he thought he would refuse. But then he remembered his promise to Our Lord all those years ago in his hut in the woods, when he had said, "Lord, I will do whatever Thou dost desire." So he wiped away his tears and sent a reply to the Pope, saying he was on his way to Bourges.

Per

A bishop is a Prince of the Church, so, like a prince of a kingdom, he has to live in a grand palace and have lots of servants and be treated with the utmost honor. When William became the Archbishop of Bourges, he had no choice but to accept these things. Yet in his heart he still thought of himself as nothing but a poor and lowly Cistercian monk, even though he could no longer wear his beloved Cistercian habit. He never spent money on himself, never ate meat, and under his fancy black cassock he always wore a hairshirt, which is a special kind of vest made of itchy, prickly stuff. Many of the saints wore hairshirts as a penance, so that they would feel uncomfortable all the time, but no one else would ever know.

The people of Bourges loved their new Archbishop. He was often seen with his friendly pet dog walking through the poorest and dirtiest areas of town, carrying food from his own table to give to those who had nothing to eat. Whenever he went out like this, he gave himself permission to dress in his old white Cistercian habit, which he loved so much. Seeing him wear it helped the people think of him as one of them, and not as their mighty Archbishop.

William would visit the sick too, and bring them medicine and wash their wounds with his own hands. William always had a treat or saint picture in his pocket to give to the children. His huge dog followed him everywhere, and the children loved to play with it. Sometimes God even let William work miracles and cure people by his prayers.

Many years passed. William was pleased he could help so many of God's suffering children. But one thing made him very sad, and that was the thought of all the people in pagan lands, who had never even heard of Our Lord Jesus Christ and had no idea how to go about saving their souls. William wanted more than anything to travel to them and teach them the Catholic faith.

So one day he got very daring and decided to write to the Pope. In his letter, he asked the Pope if he could stop living in France and go to faraway lands as a missionary priest. He was sure the Pope would say no, but he sent the letter anyhow and waited with hope for an answer.

Finally the awaited letter came with the Pope's answer. To William's great astonishment, the answer was yes! He was allowed to leave France and become a missionary priest!

William was overjoyed. He excitedly took off his black cassock and put back on his white habit. (It was a good thing he still had it, because most missionaries need to wear white anyhow.)

But, while William was joyfully making all his arrangements to leave, God was planning one last HUGE surprise. You see, it wasn't God's will at all that William become a missionary in a faraway pagan land. Instead, Our Lord was about to take him somewhere most unexpected . . . and that was to be the most wonderful place ever, which is Heaven!

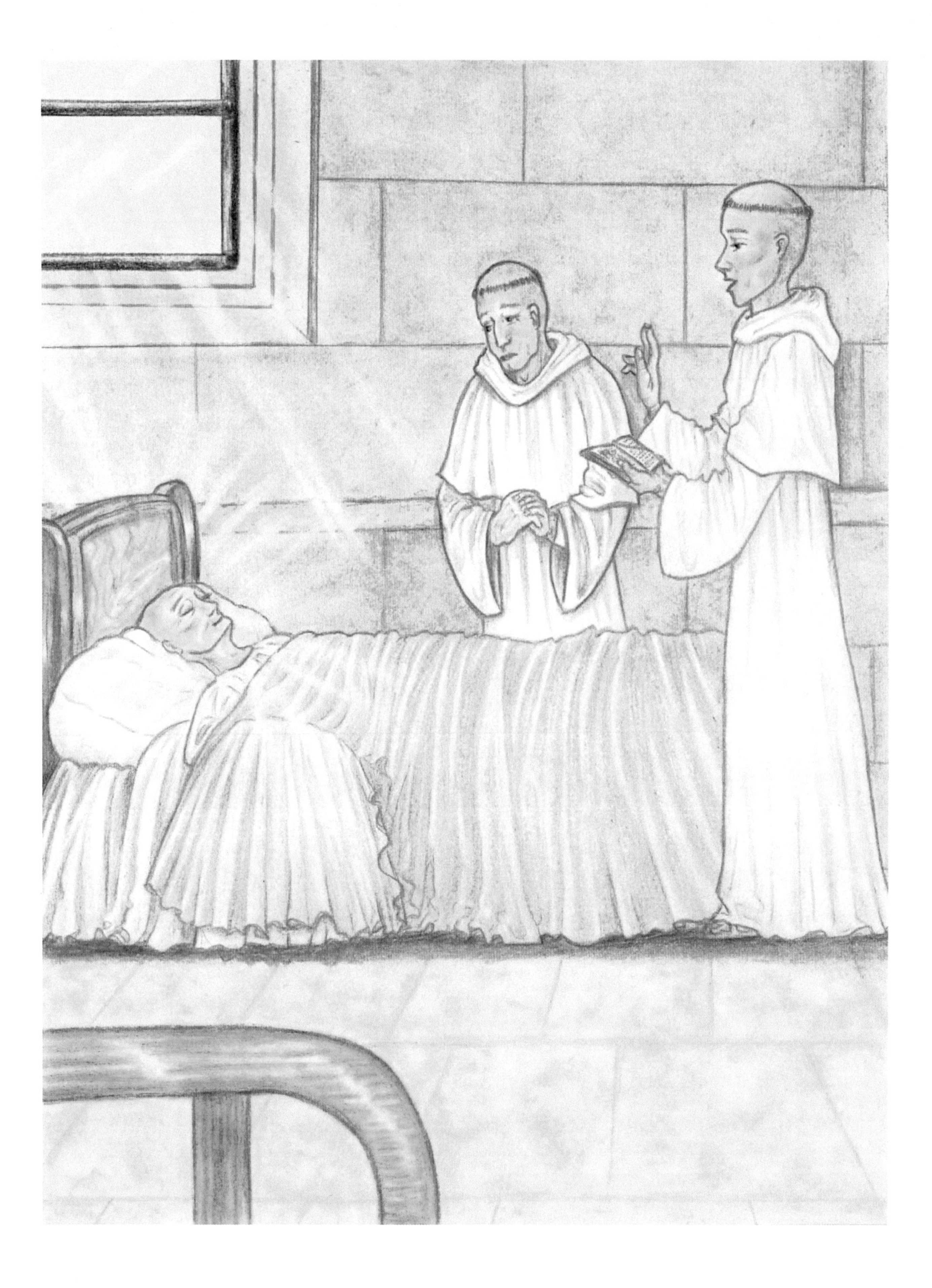

All of a sudden, William got sick. At first he thought it was just a little cold or a flu, but soon he realized that he was actually dying! He asked another priest for Extreme Unction, which he received with great love and resignation to God's holy will.

Shortly afterwards he died and his soul flew straight to Heaven, where he has been ever since. Finally he gets to stay in one place for the rest of eternity!

Saint William loves it when people pray to him . . . and if you ask him to help you become holy, you never know what wonderful surprises you might get!

His Feast Day is January 10. Saint William, pray for us!

The End

<u>Books by Susan Peek</u>

Young Adult Novels:

"God's Forgotten Friends: Lives of Little-known Saints" Series

A Soldier Surrenders: The Conversion of St. Camillus de Lellis
Crusader King: A Novel of Baldwin IV and the Crusades
Saint Magnus, The Last Viking
The King's Prey: Saint Dymphna of Ireland

* * * * *

Children's Books (Illustrated by Martina Parnelli):

"God's Forgotten Friends for Children" Series

Small for the Glory of God: St. John the Dwarf
The Man God Kept Surprising: St. William of Bourges
The Forgotten Christmas Saint: St. Anastasia

"Animals of God" Series

Animals of God, Volume 1
Animals of God, Volume 2

"Saint Rudolph and the Reindeer" **(Illustrated by Anne Peek)**

About the Author

Susan Peek is a wife, mother of eleven children, and a Third Order Franciscan. Her passion is writing novels of obscure saints and heroes, especially for teens. She is an active member of the Catholic Writers' Guild and is currently working on two parallel series: *"God's Forgotten Friends: Lives of Little-known Saints,"* for young adults, and *"God's Forgotten Friends for Children,"* of which this book is the third. Her other books for children include *Animals of God, Volumes One and Two,* also illustrated by Martina Parnelli, and *Saint Rudolph and the Reindeer*, illustrated by Anne Peek.
You can visit her at www.susanpeekauthor.com.

About the Illustrator

Artist and writer Martina Parnelli resides in western Michigan where she enjoys learning about the local flora and teaching the chickadees to eat from her hand. She takes an interest in matters historical and medicinal, as well as all things relating to home craft. As an author, she has written numerous poems, some stories and several plays. She also enjoys composing music. Her books for children include *"Fat John, His Little Lamb, and the Two Wise Owls"* co-authored with M. Roberto Angelorum and published by Leonine Publishers. Her delightful *Little Runty* series tells the accounts of the Holy Family with the donkey that was with them at Bethlehem. And her adult/ teens books *Who Shall Wear the Wedding Veil?* and *Love's Labour Started* are available as well through her website: www.martinaparnelliauthor.com

Did you know that reviews sell books?

If you have enjoyed this story, or other books by Susan Peek or Martina Parnelli,

please consider posting a brief review on Amazon, Goodreads, or your favorite book site.

Even a sentence or two would make the authors so happy!

Thank you and God bless!

Made in the USA
Columbia, SC
29 September 2020

21378284R00024